MANAGING MENTA

Managing OCD

Craig E. Blohm

ReferencePoint
Press®

San Diego, CA

© 2022 ReferencePoint Press, Inc.
Printed in the United States

For more information, contact:
ReferencePoint Press, Inc.
PO Box 27779
San Diego, CA 92198
www.ReferencePointPress.com

LIBRARY OF CONGRESS CATALOGING-IN-PUBLICATION DATA

Names: Blohm, Craig E., 1948- author.
Title: Managing OCD / by Craig E. Blohm.
Description: San Diego, CA : ReferencePoint Press, Inc., 2022. | Series: Managing mental health
Identifiers: LCCN 2021018497 (print) | LCCN 2021018498 (ebook) | ISBN 9781678201081
     (library binding) | ISBN 9781678201098 (ebook)
Subjects: LCSH: Obsessive-compulsive disorder--Treatment--Juvenile literature. |
     Obsessive-compulsive disorder in children--Treatment--Juvenile literature.
Classification: LCC RC533 .B56 2022 (print) | LCC RC533 (ebook) | DDC 616.85/22700835--dc23
LC record available at https://lccn.loc.gov/2021018497
LC ebook record available at https://lccn.loc.gov/2021018498

Contents

Ben's Story

Ben was about eight years old when the fearful thoughts began. He worried that his parents were going to abandon him and he would have to spend his life alone. To ease these fears, Ben created ritual behaviors such as touching certain things or saying certain words that, in his mind, would prevent his parents from leaving. "If I touch this Mom and Dad won't leave, it will be okay,"[1] he thought. His parents noticed these behaviors and grew concerned. They took him to a therapist, and for a while Ben seemed better.

But by the time he was about twelve years old, things got worse. He felt that there was a "dragon" in his head, tormenting him. "I'd be trying to get out of a room," Ben recalls, "and I'm touching frantically, especially when I'm scared about something, like if Mom and Dad were going out to dinner, I mean, I had to touch everything for them to come home safely."[2]

Ben's need to constantly reassure himself that nothing bad would happen was interfering with his school, sports, and home life. His sister pleaded, "I want the old Ben back; I want you to be okay again."[3]

Obsessions and Compulsions

Ben is not alone in his struggle against distressing thoughts and the belief that certain actions will get rid of them. He suffers from obsessive-compulsive disorder

(OCD), a mental illness that affects about one in forty adults and one in one hundred children in the United States. The disorder is characterized by two major aspects, which give it its name: obsessions, which are recurring unwanted thoughts, urges, or mental images that cause a person anxiety and distress; and compulsions, repetitive behaviors that a person feels compelled to perform. OCD sufferers experience obsessions, compulsions, or both at the same time, and they may also suffer from other conditions, such as severe depression.

Obsessions and compulsions vary from person to person, but some are fairly common in people with OCD. Obsessive thoughts can include worries about harming a loved one, fear of germs, fear of accidentally causing a disaster such as a fire or auto accident, or like Ben, fear of being abandoned. Compulsions can include repeated checking of door locks or stove burners, constant counting of things, excessive hand washing, and hoarding that results in a dangerously cluttered home. Obsessions and compulsions can be triggered by physical events: for example, witnessing a car accident might activate the fear that a person might inadvertently cause a similar crash. Mental triggers such as remembering a previous uncomfortable or embarrassing situation may also prompt an OCD compulsion.

> "I'd be trying to get out of a room and I'm touching frantically, especially when I'm scared about something, like if Mom and Dad were going out to dinner, I mean, I had to touch everything for them to come home safely."[2]
>
> —Ben, a youth with OCD

OCD Is Treatable

Many people with OCD find their obsessive or compulsive behavior embarrassing and shameful, which often results in the denial that there is anything wrong. Some become adept at hiding their symptoms, essentially living a double life: minimizing their OCD symptoms in public, while indulging them when they are alone.

Although there is no cure for OCD, its symptoms can be managed. Therapy and medication are the two primary methods used by mental health professionals to treat patients with OCD. Psychological counseling can help OCD sufferers understand that their obsessive thoughts are not their fault and that they can overcome them. Eventually, patients learn to tolerate these thoughts and to reject the fears they cause. Compulsions can be minimized by therapy that exposes OCD sufferers to things that trigger their symptoms but prevents them from performing the ritualistic actions they normally use to relieve their anxiety.

Medication is also used to treat the symptoms of OCD. A class of drugs known as selective serotonin reuptake inhibitors (SSRIs) has been found to be very effective in many people with OCD. Usually prescribed for people with depression, SSRIs help control a chemical called serotonin, which facilitates communication within the brain. When serotonin levels are too low, OCD can occur. SSRIs raise these levels, which helps alleviate the symptoms.

The obsessions and compulsions of OCD vary from person to person, but some are fairly common. Common compulsions include excessive hand washing and repeated checking of door locks or house alarms.

OCD is a lifelong challenge. Therapist and OCD sufferer Shala Nicely says, "It's chronic. For the majority of people, once you have OCD, you'll probably always have it."[4] OCD symptoms can vary in intensity over a lifetime, sometimes becoming so mild that the disorder seems to have disappeared, then worsening into a condition that seems to make a normal life impossible. With treatment, even these shifting intensity levels can be managed.

> "For the majority of people, once you have OCD, you'll probably always have it."[4]
>
> —Shala Nicely, therapist

Ben's journey through the fears and anxieties of OCD is a success story. By the time he was seventeen, medication and therapy had turned the fearful twelve-year-old into a confident young man who could enjoy school, sports, friends and family, and even travel abroad by himself. He has mentored other kids with OCD, telling his story and giving them hope that they, too, can conquer the dragon in their head.

Chapter One

What Is OCD?

The human brain is a constantly active thought-creating machine. A 2020 study by psychologists at Queen's University in Canada estimated that the brain produces more than six thousand thoughts per day in healthy adults. That is almost four hundred individual thoughts occurring every waking hour. These thoughts can range from deep philosophical questions and creative insights that inspire great art or literature to mundane decisions such as what outfit to wear to school or work. For most people, such thoughts are fleeting and are soon replaced by newer ones as their day progresses. There are, however, people who experience troubling thoughts that they find impossible to ignore.

Intrusive Thoughts

Among the thoughts that people have every day are ideas and images known as intrusive thoughts, which can seem to pop into the consciousness suddenly out of nowhere. They are not prompted by an external event but simply appear, unwanted, in a person's consciousness. Intrusive thoughts can be deceptive because they often seem believable. Emma has suffered from intrusive thoughts since age four. "These thoughts are clever," she says, "because the voice they are spoken in sounds like your own; they are convincing, realistic (to you) and almost always very distressing."[5] Although most people do not realize it, having troubling thoughts is a common occurrence. An international study conducted by psychologist Adam Radomsky and published in the *Journal of Obsessive-Compulsive and Related Disorders* found that 94 percent of subjects indicated that they have had unwanted thoughts at one time or another.

Intrusive thoughts are disturbing and can be bizarre, blasphemous, sexually inappropriate, or include mental images of aggressive or violent behavior. The Anxiety and Depression Association of America reports that some 6 million people in the United States are distressed by such thoughts. Although most people are able to ignore these thoughts, for others the thoughts become "stuck" in their mind, creating a loop of never-ending torment. As therapist Shala Nicely explains, "[Most people] don't notice them, or they notice them and think, 'Wow, that was weird. Wonder what I could have for lunch today?' and go on with their life. People with untreated OCD, however, will have an intrusive thought and think, "Wait! Why did I have that thought? That's a horrible thought! I don't want that! I wouldn't do that! I wish these thoughts would go away!'"[6]

For Maya, intrusive thoughts began at an early age. "I experienced several irrational fears as a child," she says, "like the fears of flying, losing baby teeth, and skeletons. In elementary school, I began worrying about my family and me getting hurt. . . . For the first time contamination obsessions entered my head. . . . I was so frightened and didn't know what was wrong with me."[7] When individuals like Maya can no longer tolerate their mental anxiety and feel compelled to do something about it, their intrusive thoughts become a symptom of a more serious, chronic mental illness: obsessive-compulsive disorder (OCD).

> "[Intrusive] thoughts are clever because the voice they are spoken in sounds like your own; they are convincing, realistic (to you) and almost always very distressing."[5]
>
> —Emma, OCD sufferer

Obsessions

Maya's disturbing thoughts are a classic symptom of OCD, which affects about 2.3 million Americans. Symptoms of the disorder generally begin between ages eighteen and twenty-five, but they can start at any time, even as soon as early childhood. Symptoms normally occur gradually at the onset of the disorder, becoming worse with age. While these symptoms are often mild, as many as half of adults who suffer from OCD experience symptoms that create serious impairment to the quality of life.

The name OCD embodies the two aspects of the disorder: obsessions and compulsions. Obsessions are unwelcome thoughts or images that are upsetting to the person who experiences them. The fifth edition of the *Diagnostic and Statistical Manual of Mental Disorders* (DSM-5) is the primary reference used by mental health professionals in diagnosing mental illness. The DSM-5 describes obsessions as "recurrent and persistent thoughts, urges, or images that are experienced, at some time

Intrusive, or unwanted, thoughts are not unusual but most people can ignore them. In people with OCD, these thoughts become—in a sense—stuck in a continuous loop.

during the disturbance, as intrusive and unwanted, and that in most individuals cause marked anxiety or distress."[8]

Obsessions can take many forms. One of the most common obsessions is a fear of contamination, in which a person with OCD is unreasonably afraid of dirt, germs, or other contaminants. This obsession may include being harmed by bodily fluids, waste, insects, various household cleaning products, and other items that sufferers are worried will make them sick. OCD sufferers with this obsession may also believe that they are capable of contaminating others. Aggressive thoughts centered on causing harm to someone, or harming oneself, are another common obsession. Someone with OCD may have thoughts about deliberately harming or killing a coworker, schoolmate, or even a complete stranger. A babysitter may feel fearful about hurting the child he or she is caring for, perhaps drowning the child in the bathtub or shaking the child to death.

Doubt can play a role in obsessions. Many people with OCD become preoccupied with the idea that a certain task they were responsible for doing has not been done or has been done incorrectly. This can include doubts about performing job duties, household chores, care of family members, or school homework assignments. In a strange form of OCD, the sufferer thinks that a particularly vivid thought could actually be a memory of a violent act he or she has already committed. Such ambiguity causes great anxiety in the person with such thoughts.

People with OCD may experience obsessions concerning religious or moral issues. These can manifest as a fear of loss of self-control, such as shouting profanities in church or thinking blasphemous thoughts during prayer. They may also worry that they will have a sudden urge to do something that goes against

> "People with untreated OCD, however, will have an intrusive thought and think, 'Wait! Why did I have that thought? That's a horrible thought! I don't want that! I wouldn't do that! I wish these thoughts would go away!'"[6]
>
> —Shala Nicely, therapist

What OCD Is Like

For people who do not have OCD, it is difficult to understand what an OCD sufferer is going through. Clinical definitions found on the internet are inadequate in conveying the intrusive reality of the obsessions and compulsions of the disorder. Cheryl Little Sutton, who has OCD, vividly describes the condition on the Facebook page of the International OCD Foundation, a nonprofit organization that helps OCD sufferers:

> Picture standing in a room filled with flies and pouring a bottle of syrup over yourself. The flies constantly swarm about you, buzzing around your head and in your face. You swat and swat, but they keep coming. The flies are like obsessional thoughts—you can't stop them, you just have to fend them off. The swatting is like compulsions—you can't resist the urge to do it, even though you know it won't really keep the flies at bay more than for a brief moment.

Quoted in Tyler Dabel, "Living with OCD: What It's Actually Like," Bridges to Recovery, November 21, 2016. www.bridgestorecovery.com.

their moral principles, perhaps shoplifting, cheating on a spouse, or taking credit for someone else's work.

Obsessing over superstitious thoughts is another aspect of OCD. Sufferers may consider certain numbers, words, sayings, or colors to be lucky or able to prevent bad things from happening. Casual superstitions are common: about half of all Americans admit to being at least somewhat superstitious. A casual superstition, such as always wearing a "lucky" shirt while engaging in a sport, can be fun. But when people with OCD fixate on such talismans in the belief that they actually ward off evil or failure, it becomes more than just a harmless quirk.

There is a common belief that people who are perfectionists are exhibiting symptoms of OCD. But the two are actually different. While a perfectionist feels the need to do everything a certain way and is not satisfied with less than flawlessness, this is a personality trait and not a mental disorder like OCD. The difference lies in the underlying motives for perfectionism. The website Modern Therapy concisely describes this difference: A perfectionist says, "I have to make sure every screw is tightened all the way.

(*So that my bike is safe and functions efficiently.*)" An OCD sufferer says, "I have to make sure every screw is tightened all the way. (*So I don't die.*)"[9]

People with OCD often realize that their fixations on unwanted thoughts is not normal but are unable to stop obsessing over them. Instead, they try to find ways to alleviate the anxiety brought on by their intrusive thoughts. These coping methods are called compulsions.

Compulsions

Compulsions are repetitive actions that people with OCD feel they must perform in order to reduce the anxiety brought on by an obsession. These actions are not enjoyable for the person, and they do not accomplish any useful goals. Although many, if not most, OCD sufferers realize that their compulsions will not completely rid them of their obsessions, they find that these rituals provide a needed, although temporary, relief. But giving in to compulsions can drastically disrupt a person's daily life, as well as add the stress of feeling forced to perform actions that they would rather not engage in.

Maya's obsessions worsened as she grew older. She developed social anxiety in middle school, and by the time she entered high school, she began experiencing a new obsession: she became irrationally afraid of becoming contaminated. Like most people with OCD, she began to devise rituals to ease her anxiety. Her fear of dirt and other impurities led Maya to take numerous long showers and scrub her hands raw, trying to get rid of every bit of contamination. The compulsion of excessive washing is one of the most common impulses in people with OCD and is the one most often found in children and adolescents.

"In elementary school, I began worrying about my family and me getting hurt. . . . I was so frightened and didn't know what was wrong with me."[7]

—Maya, OCD sufferer

While hand washing is an important part of a daily health

In people with OCD, an obsession with dirt and germs is often accompanied by extreme fear of somehow contaminating other people. To cope with this obsession, these individuals often resort to repeated hand washing.

routine, OCD sufferers take it to extremes, washing their hands over and over again, often twenty or thirty times or more in a row. In extreme cases, an OCD sufferer may wash more than two hundred times a day. Cleaning compulsions can also involve changing clothes frequently, discarding perfectly good items that are feared to be contaminated, or being overly meticulous in sanitizing one's home environment or place of work. Only when they feel truly clean can people with OCD move past the obsession to resume their normal daily activities.

Compulsions may involve certain rituals or repetitive physical actions that are believed to counteract obsessions. Walking a certain number of steps, for example, or being careful not to step on cracks in the sidewalk are ritualistic compulsions common to OCD. Some people with OCD will touch a chair or sofa a certain number of times before sitting or tap on a door frame in a particular pattern before entering a room.

Another sign of OCD involves an uncontrollable need to count things. The counting compulsion can include physical objects such as books on a shelf or hangers in a closet or less tangible things like footsteps, breaths, eyeblinks, ticks made by a clock, and words (or even syllables) being spoken. Some OCD sufferers may compulsively assign the qualitative attributes of "good" or "bad" to various things. For example, even numbers may be considered good, while odd numbers are bad; the color red can be bad, while blue is good.

OCD leads many people to be plagued by nagging doubts, usually about things such as whether they have turned off the stove or electrical appliances, locked all doors before leaving the house or retiring for the night, or checked to see that all their possessions are stored in their proper places. Such obsessions can lead to a compulsion called checking. With this compulsion, OCD sufferers may check door locks dozens of times or touch each knob on a stove again and again to make sure everything has been done to prevent an imagined catastrophe, such as a burglary or house fire. Compulsive checking may also include reviewing business projects or schoolwork—multiple times—to be sure that assignments have been completed correctly. People with OCD may also have doubts concerning their personal worthiness and may seek frequent reassurance of their value as a person. Such constant displays of neediness can isolate OCD sufferers from the people closest to them, resulting in alienation from family, friends, and coworkers.

Many OCD sufferers exhibit more than one compulsion, such as a person who obsessively counts, arranges objects, and also performs hand-washing rituals. Sometimes a compulsion will diminish or disappear, only to be replaced by another.

People with OCD perform compulsions not because they bring pleasure (they do not) but because not doing them would be unbearable. Of course, performing compulsive behaviors will not in any way affect an obsession: arranging clothes in a certain order in a closet has no effect on whether a person becomes ill or is hurt in an accident. Most OCD sufferers understand this, but they are still powerless to stop the actions that reduce their anxiety.

OCD and Related Disorders

A particularly distressing and rare form of OCD is called purely (or primarily) obsessional OCD, often referred to as Pure OCD or Pure O. In this subtype of OCD, the unwanted thoughts that enter a person's mind are extremely personal, centering on the core values of that person's concept of self. Because of this close relation to a person's basic beliefs and morals, Pure O can lead to extreme anxiety.

The unwelcome thoughts in Pure O may be religious in nature, such as obsessions provoking fears that a person will do something sacrilegious, thereby offending God. They may involve visions of violent acts being performed against loved ones (sometimes categorized as "harm OCD") or have a sexual component such as fear of becoming a rapist or pedophile. These thoughts can be so forceful that they cause a person to have grave doubts as to the possibility of actually doing such abhorrent actions.

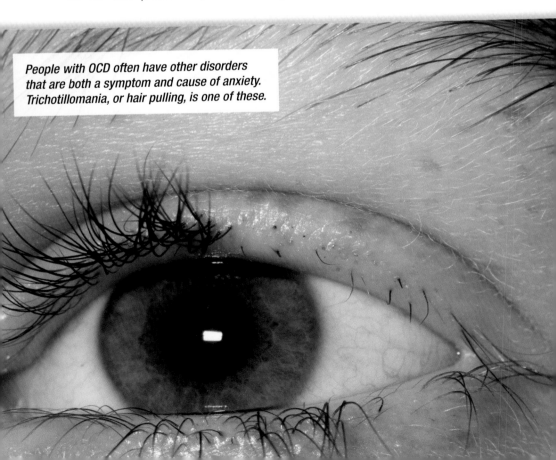

People with OCD often have other disorders that are both a symptom and cause of anxiety. Trichotillomania, or hair pulling, is one of these.

People who are highly organized, seek perfection in everything they do, are thrifty to a fault, and strictly adhere to the most minute rules and regulations may seem to be a perfect example of an OCD sufferer. But they could instead be suffering from a similar form of obsessional disorder known as obsessive-compulsive personality disorder, or OCPD.

The symptoms of OCPD are similar to those of OCD. But it is the details behind the symptoms that distinguish these two disorders from each other. People with OCD often feel shame and guilt in connection with their obsessive thoughts and the compulsions they perform to ease their anxiety. People with OCPD, on the other hand, exude a moral confidence that the way they do things is the only correct way, and everyone else should live up to their example. While OCD sufferers perform rituals to prevent bad consequences of their thoughts, those with OCPD have no such negative considerations. They like themselves and how they perform in the world.

Studies about OCPD are limited, and no cause has yet been identified. Genetics, environment, and a strict upbringing may all play a part in the origin of this disorder.

What-if thinking abounds in people with Pure OCD: "What if I am really capable of doing these things? What if my personality or my morals have somehow changed to permit me to even think such awful thoughts? What if I am really an evil person?"

The DSM-5 does not include a special category for this form of the disorder, but there are differences between typical OCD and Pure O. In Pure O the tactics sufferers use to relieve their anxiety remain internal and not visible to the outside world. Instead of, say, repeatedly washing their hands or arranging books on a shelf, individuals with Pure O perform mental compulsions to relieve their anxiety. For example, a person thinking about harming a loved one may counteract this obsession by mentally repeating assurances that he or she would not actually hurt the individual. Other mental compulsions may include hoping that superstitions or "magical thinking" will relieve the obsessions, silently repeating special calming words over and over, mentally counting, or making mental lists. Because of its lack of outward signs, Pure O is often misunderstood by both sufferers and their acquaintances, and it can be difficult for professionals to diagnose.

Many people with OCD experience other disorders as well. There are several psychological conditions that are related to OCD and can increase anxiety in the OCD sufferer. In body dysmorphic disorder (BDD), a person is obsessed with one or more perceived defects of his or her own appearance. People with BDD may believe that their body is unattractive, either too obese or too thin, or that they have flaws that other people find ugly or abnormal. According to the DSM-5, sufferers of BDD may exhibit compulsions such as excessively looking in a mirror, applying makeup to hide a perceived fault, grooming excessively, or even resorting to cosmetic surgery to change their appearance.

Trichotillomania (hair pulling) and excoriation (skin picking) are two disorders that may also accompany OCD. Both can damage an individual's appearance and health and cause an increase in anxiety.

For those who do not suffer from it, OCD is often dismissed as nothing more than a peculiar quirk. Someone who is temporarily fixating on something may flippantly say, "Wow, I've really got OCD today!" Movies and television may portray OCD as a harmless or even humorous idiosyncrasy. But, as true sufferers of OCD know, it is an all-too-real mental illness that can make everyday life intolerable.

Chapter Two

The Causes of OCD

The obsessions and compulsions of OCD are naturally very disconcerting to sufferers, and many blame themselves for the anxiety and embarrassment the disorder causes. But researchers believe that OCD may be caused by a combination of physical, genetic, and psychological factors. They suggest that one explanation for how a person develops OCD lies within the incredibly sophisticated human brain.

Weighing in at about 3 pounds (1.36 kg), the brain is a marvel of power and complexity. Some 100 billion nerve cells called neurons are continually sending electrical signals racing through the brain, controlling the body's physical actions, stimulating emotions and memories, and generating thoughts. They also deliver messages that interpret what is happening in a person's environment and how to respond to stimuli. This constant communication generally works so well, carrying out millions of tasks every second, that most people take the brain's awesome capabilities for granted. But in some individuals, something goes wrong with the process of transferring information through the brain. This can lead to a number of mental disorders, including OCD.

The human brain has two hemispheres, each divided into four main lobes—frontal, parietal, occipital, and temporal—that control various functions of the body. Scientists believe that a problem in nerve communication between two regions of the brain plays a part in whether a person has OCD. The orbitofrontal cortex is an area at the very front of the brain that has a role in controlling social behavior, reward experience (for example, knowing that eating a delicious meal will bring pleasure), and most importantly for OCD sufferers, decision-making. While relatively little is understood about this area of the brain, researchers know that there is a connection between the orbitofrontal cortex and a cluster of neurons called the basal ganglia. Located deep inside the brain, the basal ganglia help regulate basic motor functions, as well as knowledge, understanding, and emotions.

"In OCD, the brain responds too much to errors, and too little to stop signals, abnormalities that researchers had suspected to play a crucial role in OCD."[10]

—Luke Norman, psychiatric researcher

In people with OCD, the normal pattern of communication between these two areas of the brain becomes hyperactive. This causes a part of the basal ganglia called the caudate nucleus to send too many messages to the orbitofrontal cortex, which becomes overwhelmed and thus is hindered in its decision-making. It cannot determine which messages are important enough to require a physical response and which are okay to ignore. This can overwhelm the OCD sufferer's brain, triggering a state of uncertainty: the knowledge that he or she locked the front door before leaving the house is contradicted by the fear that the door was not really locked after all. This uncertainty within the brain triggers a loop of recurring obsession, causing overwhelming anxiety. Typical thoughts might be like this: "I know I locked the door, but my brain is telling me I didn't. What if my brain is right? I need to go back and check, but then I'll be late for work. I might get fired, but if I don't check the door, a burglar may come in and steal my stuff." Such anxiety can occur in people with OCD in any number of situations, including locking doors, turning off appliances, making sure items are stored in proper order, and maintaining personal and environmental cleanliness.

Brain scans have confirmed the role of functional brain abnormalities in OCD sufferers. In 2018 a study at the University of Michigan compared functional magnetic resonance imaging (fMRI) scans of people with and without OCD. The study confirmed that irregularities in the brain's communication system are an underlying cause of OCD. According to Luke Norman, the lead author of the study, "These results show that, in OCD, the brain responds too much to errors, and too little to stop signals, abnormalities that researchers had suspected to play a crucial role in OCD, but that had not been conclusively shown. . . . [In this study] we could see how brain circuits long hypothesized to be crucial to OCD are indeed involved in the disorder."[10]

Imaging has revealed structural differences in the brains of OCD patients as well. Gray matter, which processes information, makes up about 40 percent of the human brain. In individuals

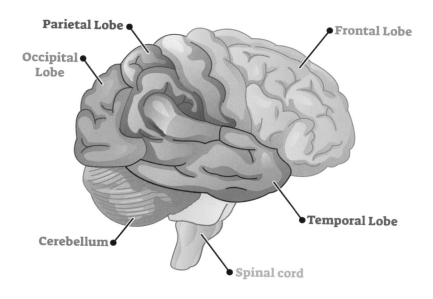

The human brain has two hemispheres, each divided into four main lobes—frontal, parietal, occipital, and temporal. These lobes control various functions of the body. They may also contain clues to understanding the causes of OCD.

Parietal Lobe

Frontal Lobe

Occipital Lobe

Temporal Lobe

Cerebellum

Spinal cord

Modern science allows researchers to look into the far reaches of the universe with an orbiting telescope and examine the building blocks of matter using an electron microscope. Employing a technology called functional magnetic resonance imaging, doctors have looked into the human brain in their search for a physical basis for OCD.

Magnetic resonance imaging, or MRI, uses powerful magnetic fields to record images of organs inside the body. These images help doctors diagnose illnesses that are not visible by simple observation. A functional MRI (fMRI) records the real-time function of the brain rather than just the structure, aiding researchers in pinpointing possible abnormal activity that can cause disorders such as OCD. Because MRI scans use magnetic fields, they are generally safer for the patient than computed tomography (CT) scans, which use radiation that can be harmful with repeated exposure.

An fMRI scan identifies brain activity that can cause OCD, as well as other mental disorders such as attention-deficit/hyperactivity disorder, depression, schizophrenia, anorexia, and other illnesses. It can also help determine the causes of other diseases, such as brain tumors, and neurological problems such as Alzheimer's disease or dementia.

with OCD, scans found an increase in the density of the gray matter in the orbitofrontal cortex. This finding is consistent with the idea that hyperactivity in this region of the brain is associated with OCD.

A Genetic Connection

Scientists also believe that genetics plays a role in the development of OCD. Genes are portions of deoxyribonucleic acid, or DNA, located on chromosomes within the nucleus of each cell in the body. They carry specific characteristics that are passed from parents to offspring and determine numerous traits such as eye and hair color, height, temperament, intelligence, and many other attributes that combine to make a person a unique individual. Genes may also determine whether a person is susceptible to a particular disease, such as cystic fibrosis, muscular dystrophy, Huntington's disease, and some cancers. Researchers have long assumed that OCD has a genetic component that makes it an inheritable disease, but the specific genes involved have been difficult to find.

In 2017 scientists discovered evidence of OCD's genetic connection. Working with the Massachusetts Institute of Technology and Harvard University, researchers studied some six hundred genes (out of the approximately thirty thousand genes in the human genome) to determine whether any of them play a role in the development of OCD. These genes came not only from humans but from mice and dogs as well, since these animals often exhibit compulsive actions. "Dogs, it turns out, are surprisingly similar to people," says geneticist Elinor Karlsson. "They're chasing their own tail or chewing themselves or chasing shadows like normal, but they're doing it for hours. They literally can't stop."[11] The human test subjects included people both with and without OCD.

Out of the approximately six hundred genes studied, researchers did not locate a specific gene responsible for OCD. They did, however, identify four genes that are closely associated with the disorder. The study reported that abnormalities in these four genes can disrupt the neural communication within the brain, specifically between the orbitofrontal cortex and the caudate nucleus, where garbled messages can trigger obsessive and compulsive behavior. This confirmed that susceptibility to OCD can be passed from a parent to a child. "We know you're four times more likely to develop OCD if you have a first-degree relative with the disorder,"[12] notes Jessica Griffin, a psychology professor at the University of New South Wales in Australia.

"We know you're four times more likely to develop OCD if you have a first-degree relative with the disorder."[12]

—Jessica Griffin, psychology professor

But genetics is only part of the picture when it comes to OCD. "Genetics contribute to overall risk," says Christopher Pittenger, director of Yale University's OCD Research Clinic, "but they do not completely determine whether or not an individual is going to develop the disorder."[13] Other factors also have an influence on the development of this complicated disorder.

Environmental Impacts on OCD

Throughout history, psychologists have debated a question about human behavior that can be summed up in the phrase "nature versus nurture." This phrase suggests two ways of understanding the presence of some personality traits or a predisposition to certain illnesses. Are they caused by genetics (nature) or by factors in the environment in which a person lives (nurture)? There are many examples that demonstrate how both of these factors can be important for human development. If a child's parents are tall, for instance, that child may inherit the gene for increased height. But if that child grows up in an environment where, say, nutrition is inadequate, that child may not grow to the height coded in his or her genes.

In the case of OCD, genetics plays a role in determining the likelihood of developing the disorder, but environment also has an impact. For example, drug use has been shown to increase the risk of a person developing OCD. Trauma to the brain due to injury or certain types of child abuse can damage the structure and communication ability of a child's brain, leading to OCD symptoms later in life. Even navigating the everyday pressures of life or suffering psychological distress can contribute to an individual's OCD. "Contributing factors," notes Ohio State University psychologist Cheryl Carmin, "are 'triggers' such as overwhelming stress or a traumatic event (a family reunion, for instance, or seeing a dead mouse) that might bring on OCD symptoms."[14] Other triggers (sometimes called stressors) can include things as harmless as being a bit late for an appointment or missing a bus or as life-changing as losing a job, ending a relationship, or the death of a loved one. For one OCD sufferer, the simple (and necessary) act of eating caused great anxiety. She had to eat alone because hearing someone cough or belch while she was eating brought on a fear of choking. Her OCD made her have dinner at precisely 6:00 p.m.—no earlier, no later.

Uncertainty within the brain can trigger a loop of recurring obsession that then causes overwhelming anxiety. This anxiety can lead to any number of compulsive behaviors, including checking and rechecking that items are stored in a particular order.

Many families with an OCD-afflicted child may contribute to the problems caused by the disorder without even understanding that they are doing so. If, for example, a child exhibits excessive hand washing due to fear of contamination, the parents might accommodate this compulsion by keeping the child's surroundings as clean as possible and making sure that there is plenty of soap available for the child to use. While this may temporarily relieve the child's anxiety, experts say it reinforces the false notion that performing rituals is a valid way to deal with an obsession.

While psychological and social factors can contribute to the onset of OCD, another environmental trigger involves a particular infection in children. This type of early onset OCD is known as PANDAS, and it has nothing to do with cute furry bears.

PANDAS in Children

The term *PANDAS* stands for "pediatric autoimmune neuropsychiatric disorders associated with streptococcus." This group of highly technical words describes a type of OCD that can appear after a child has gotten over an illness, usually a streptococcal bacteria infection that causes strep throat or scarlet fever. PANDAS can occur as early as age three; it is rare after a child reaches adolescence. Many doctors believe that antibodies created by the human immune system to fight invading strep bacteria may also attack healthy cells in the brain, causing OCD.

Parents are usually the first to notice sudden dramatic changes in a child's behavior that indicate PANDAS. Shortly after recovering from a streptococcal infection, a child may begin to exhibit the classic obsession and compulsion symptoms of OCD. In addition, other anomalies may develop, such as anxiety if separated from parents, involuntary muscle movements called tics, changes in mood, hyperactivity, and difficulty sleeping. While some of these behaviors are common at certain stages of child development, their appearance immediately after a strep infection strongly suggests PANDAS. In cases in which the child already exhibits signs of OCD, the streptococcal infection can make them worse.

OCD and Other Mental Illnesses

Living with OCD is challenging enough, but many people with the disorder also suffer from other related mental conditions. Having two or more mental illnesses is called comorbidity, and it can make dealing with OCD more difficult.

Depression is common in OCD sufferers. Two out of three people with OCD experience a major depressive episode along with their OCD, according to clinical psychologist Owen Kelly. Depression usually occurs after a person has been living with OCD for some time, indicating that the stress of OCD can trigger depressive thoughts. Episodes of depression can, in turn, make OCD worse. Schizophrenia is another comorbid condition related to OCD. About one in four people diagnosed with schizophrenia show signs of OCD as well. Like OCD, schizophrenia is rooted in abnormalities in the function and structure of the brain, and both disorders can impair job performance, social relationships, and the overall quality of life.

Other mental conditions that have been associated with OCD include attention-deficit/hyperactivity disorder, eating disorders, panic attacks, drug or alcohol abuse, and generalized anxiety disorder. Having any of these comorbid conditions makes treating OCD more difficult and will usually lead to a longer course of treatment.

Doctors will usually prescribe antibiotics to treat a strep infection. As the antibiotics take effect and the infection disappears, the child's OCD symptoms will eventually start to subside. However, if another strep infection occurs (and it is common to experience numerous strep throat infections throughout childhood), the OCD symptoms will flare up. Some physicians have cast a certain amount of doubt on the diagnosis of PANDAS, stating that neurological factors may play more of a role than a streptococcal infection. Research into PANDAS is ongoing, with the goal of better defining the true causes of the disorder.

OCD as a Learned Behavior

The human brain is wired to learn things, from knowing how to ride a bicycle to understanding nuclear physics. But learning can also be a component of OCD compulsions. If a person with OCD is fearful of contamination, he or she notices that repeated hand washing brings relief from the anxiety of confronting dirt or other contaminants. Thus, hand washing becomes a habit in order to combat the obsession and creates a loop in which more hand washing is associated with better control over anxiety. Associating fear with a particular object can also bring on an obsessive response. If a person has had a frightening experience in the past, such as being involved in a mishap aboard an airplane, the very sight of another plane can be enough to produce anxiety. In this example, the person will learn to avoid the object that triggers an episode of OCD by opting to use a means of transportation other than an airplane, not driving by airports, or even avoiding photographs or films involving aircraft. This "learned avoidance" may begin in childhood, and if the practice continues it can reinforce obsessive behavior throughout a person's lifetime.

Sometimes an individual's upbringing or home environment will trigger the onset of OCD. For example, parents who are excessively concerned with the possibility of falling into poverty (due, perhaps, to losing a job) may transfer to the child a sense of financial insecurity. This can cause the child to begin hoarding

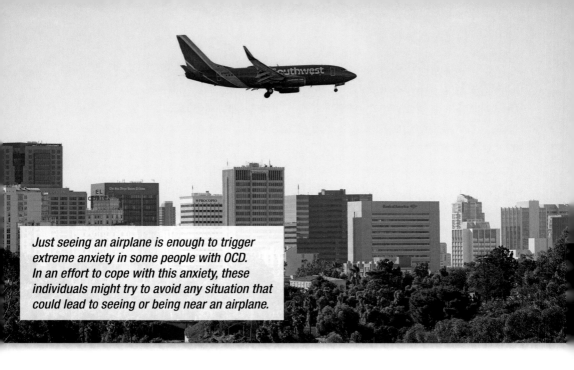

Just seeing an airplane is enough to trigger extreme anxiety in some people with OCD. In an effort to cope with this anxiety, these individuals might try to avoid any situation that could lead to seeing or being near an airplane.

things to ease the anxiety felt due to such uncertainty. Similarly, parents who are very worried about cleanliness or keeping everything tidy and orderly may create a similar obsession in their children. "My mom's a neat freak," says twelve-year-old Ally. "So am I. But arranging and rearranging my clothes for hours—that's OCD. Not being neat."[15]

Diagnosing OCD

While many people exhibit occasional mildly compulsive behavior, that does not mean such a person has OCD. But when obsessions become extreme, further investigation is called for. Kayla describes the beginning of her OCD.

> It started after my brother died. I started to worry that I would lose photos of him or letters he had written me— anything associated with him, really—little gifts he gave me when we were kids. I never threw anything away because I thought I might accidentally toss something of his away. In a few weeks, I had filled my apartment with paper and junk.

. . . I know it's crazy, but I once examined a single piece of notebook paper for over thirty minutes to make certain that something of my brother's wasn't stuck to the paper.[16]

Many people who find themselves performing obsessive rituals similar to Kayla's may be confused or believe they are going crazy. Even if they have heard of OCD, they may not think their compulsions are caused by the disorder. It often takes a friend or relative to suggest seeing a professional to obtain a proper diagnosis. It may be tempting to search the internet for advice concerning the causes and symptoms of obsessions and compulsions. But a complex disorder such as OCD requires one-on-one counseling with a doctor or qualified therapist. A visit to an individual's primary care physician is often the first step for someone seeking professional help. However, most family doctors are not trained to diagnose mental disorders. In the case of suspected OCD, the primary doctor will arrange an appointment with a mental health specialist for further evaluation.

Psychologists and psychiatrists specialize in diagnosing and treating disorders of the mind. The counselor or doctor will ask a series of questions designed to elicit information about a person's symptoms and will usually consult the DSM-5 to ascertain whether the symptoms are an indication of OCD or some other condition. Such distinctions may be difficult to diagnose. For example, someone who obsesses about food may have an eating disorder (such as anorexia or binge eating disorder) rather than OCD.

"I once examined a single piece of notebook paper for over thirty minutes to make certain that something of my brother's wasn't stuck to the paper."[16]

—Kayla, OCD sufferer

The main tool that psychiatrists and psychologists use to determine the seriousness of a patient's OCD is the second edition of the Yale-Brown Obsessive Compulsive Scale (Y-BOCS II). Administered by a mental health professional, the main part of the Y-BOCS II consists of ten questions designed to let a patient describe how much obsessive thoughts and compulsive actions interfere with his or her daily life. Answers given on a system of zero to five points for each question allow the health professional to determine the severity of the individual's OCD from none to extreme. There is also a version of the test for children.

A professional diagnosis of OCD usually brings the next logical question: can this disorder be treated or even cured? While a cure for OCD is so far elusive, there are treatments that can help an OCD sufferer a return to a relatively normal life.

Chapter Three

Treating OCD

Every day, medical science is working toward finding cures for some of the most persistent and deadly diseases known to humankind. Researchers labor tirelessly to develop new treatments for afflictions such as cancer, heart disease, and diabetes. OCD is one of the many diseases that still lack a cure. "OCD is not curable," notes therapist Shala Nicely. "I can tell you for certain—and there's not much we're certain about, as people with OCD—that you can still live a great life, even with the disorder."[17]

Cognitive Treatment

One of the most successful treatments for OCD is called cognitive behavioral therapy, or CBT. It is a form of psychotherapy that helps people deal with problems such as anxiety, depression, insomnia, post-traumatic stress disorder, and substance abuse. Treatment with CBT centers on a patient talking with a therapist for a number of weekly sessions usually over the course of several months. During these sessions, the therapist asks questions designed to discover how an individual's thoughts are affecting his or her behavior. Changing the patient's thoughts will ultimately translate into changed behavior.

Within the general area of CBT, therapists use a particular method for treating their patients with OCD. This technique, known as exposure and response prevention (ERP), involves two aspects of treatment: exposing a person to the things that trigger obsessions or intrusive thoughts and preventing the use of a compulsion to counteract the anxiety caused by the obsession. The goal for the OCD sufferer is to separate the obsession from the compulsion and ultimately acknowledge that the compulsion is not necessary to relieve the anxious feelings brought on by the obsessions. ERP is often called the "gold standard" of OCD treatment. In those who complete their treatment, says clinical psychologist Jonathan Abramowitz, it has an effectiveness rate of about 80 percent in reducing the anxiety of OCD.

"OCD is not curable, . . . [but] you can still live a great life, even with the disorder."[17]

—Shala Nicely, therapist

ERP therapy usually begins with the patient creating an exposure hierarchy, a list of the things that cause anxiety in order of severity, from the least to the most distressing. Using this list, the therapist can guide the individual gradually through confronting the least troubling to the most disturbing obsessions. In subsequent sessions, the individual begins to examine his or her obsessions and is urged by the therapist to separate those obsessions from the compulsions that are used to suppress them. This process can be difficult and even frightening for someone who may have spent a lifetime trying to cope with OCD.

Getting Her Life Back

Anne Coulter is a marketing communications consultant who suffered from unwanted thoughts and ritual behavior for years before being diagnosed with OCD. These thoughts caused her to spend hours every day performing checking rituals. Luckily, the first psychiatrist she saw recognized the telltale symptoms of the disorder. "It never occurred to me that OCD was the problem," she says. "I just thought I was losing my mind."[18] After creating her exposure hierarchy, Coulter began ERP treatments at age twenty-six. One of her obsessions was a fear of accidentally leaving a stove burner on, creating a fire hazard. Her therapist created exercises

Cognitive behavioral therapy, or CBT, has shown success in treating OCD. During therapy sessions, the therapist and patient discuss how the patient's thoughts are affecting his or her behavior and how to eventually start changing that behavior.

to help break Coulter from repeatedly checking the burner. "At first," she recalls, "I had to turn on a burner so I could see the flame, turn it off with my eyes closed, and then leave the kitchen without checking to make sure the burner was off. My therapist had me sit in the living room while my anxiety level spiked and then came down."[19] Eventually, Coulter was able to cope with turning all four burners on then off, and then without checking, leave the house and take a walk.

Other tests Coulter's therapist devised included turning on her alarm clock without repeatedly checking to see if it was set, and writing letters and emails containing missing or misspelled words, which she normally checked and rechecked numerous times before sending. After three weeks of intensive therapy, Coulter had essentially overcome her checking compulsion. For Coulter, the gold standard therapy made all the difference in her journey with OCD. "ERP gave me the tools I need to manage my OCD for the rest of my life, or at least until there's a cure. My OCD has never disappeared entirely, but now I usually think of it as an aggravation rather than a disability. . . . ERP gave me back my life."[20]

Before her ERP therapy, Coulter suffered from depression (which she did not realize was connected to her OCD). Medication helped her get through the depression so that she could benefit from her cognitive treatment. For many sufferers, medication itself can be an effective tool in their fight against OCD.

Fighting OCD with Drugs

Since OCD involves anomalies in the structure and communication system of the brain, doctors have found that certain medications can help alleviate the symptoms of the disorder. Drugs that are normally given to people who are battling depression have also shown to be effective in those with OCD. Of these drugs, the most widely prescribed are medications called selective serotonin reuptake inhibitors, or SSRIs.

Symptoms of OCD occur when communication within the brain is disrupted, so medications that help improve that communication are often prescribed. SSRIs are the most effective of these medications, creating improvement in up to 70 percent of OCD sufferers who take them. Messages travel throughout the brain in the form of electrical signals, or nerve impulses, that flow along the brain's neurons. When these signals reach a gap (called a synapse) between two neurons, they trigger a chemical neurotransmitter called serotonin to "jump" across the gap and send the communication on its way to the next neuron.

> "My OCD has never disappeared entirely, but now I usually think of it as an aggravation rather than a disability. . . . ERP gave me back my life."[20]
>
> —Anne, OCD sufferer

In normal brain communication, once the message jumps the synaptic gap, the initial neuron reabsorbs the serotonin. This process, known as reuptake, determines the length of time the serotonin remains in the gap and also recycles it to make it available

Residential Care for OCD

When outpatient sessions at a therapist's office do not create a noticeable improvement in people with severe OCD, other avenues of therapy may need to be considered. In situations in which individuals present a physical danger to themselves or others, inpatient care in a hospital provides a safe and well-monitored environment for treatment. But such treatment is only suited to short-term crisis intervention. For long-term treatment of OCD, a residential therapy program may be the answer.

At residential therapy facilities, a patient may stay from a few weeks to several months or more, depending on rate of progress and ability to afford the treatment. Treatment usually centers on ERP therapy but may also include relaxation and mindfulness techniques, guidance for proper nutrition and exercise, and medication where appropriate. A typical stay at a residential center may include therapy sessions, group encounters, weekend family visitation, exercise and leisure time, and healthy meals.

There are relatively few residential facilities around the country that deal with OCD, so for many people, travel may be required. But overcoming the anxieties of OCD and regaining a normal life is worth it for those who have not found success elsewhere.

for the next message. Doctors know that people with OCD generally have lower levels of serotonin, and this is where SSRIs play their part. In these individuals, reuptake limits the already reduced amount of serotonin available for brain communication. SSRIs are designed to inhibit the reuptake process, which increases the serotonin available and thus improves the communication between neurons and eases the symptoms of OCD. SSRIs are called "selective" because they target only serotonin rather than the many other neurotransmitters used by the body.

Most OCD sufferers who take SSRIs notice an improvement in their symptoms within about four to six weeks. Often the use of drugs combined with CBT shows better results than medication alone. A 2010–2013 Chinese study of 167 people with OCD found that "CBT combined with medication may be effective in alleviating symptoms and social functioning impairment associated with OCD, and is more effective than medication alone."[21]

For those who do not see an improvement within a few months, doctors may try augmentation therapy, in which additional medication is prescribed along with SSRIs. Augmenting an SSRI with an antipsychotic medicine has shown to be effective in many cases. Other drugs include antidepressant drugs, drugs that combat anxiety, and a class of drugs called monoamine oxidase inhibitors used for people with panic attacks and social phobias. These additional medicines can significantly improve the outcome of SSRI treatment, but they must be carefully monitored for side effects, which can include elevated cholesterol, weight gain, and uncontrolled movements of the face or body.

Of course, medication is only effective if the individual takes it. Many times the side effects of an additional drug may be severe enough to cause a patient to stop the treatment. Some OCD sufferers may be skeptical of taking drugs at all due to a contamination obsession or because they procrastinate about making the decision of whether to take the medication. In these cases, talking with a health care professional can help an OCD sufferer understand the importance of continuing their treatment.

Not all people with OCD will respond to behavioral therapy or medication. If these methods prove unsatisfactory, doctors may prescribe invasive or noninvasive brain treatments.

Probing the Brain

Twenty-eight-year-old Jon Blank suffered from severe OCD. An avid snowboarder, Blank was plagued by obsessions and compulsions that devastated his life. He repeatedly washed his hands until his knuckles bled. His numerous obsessions included a hatred of fast food and American cars and of touching anything associated with the part of the United States east of where he lives in Colorado. "I've actually lost a lot of friends," Blank says. "There's a lot of kids I used to snowboard with when I was younger. And they think I just lost my mind."[22] Failure of the traditional OCD treatments of cognitive therapy and medication made Blank an ideal candidate for a relatively new weapon against OCD: deep brain stimulation (DBS).

Used to help patients with tremors, Parkinson's disease, and other brain disorders, DBS was approved by the US Food and

Drug Administration (FDA) for use in extreme cases of OCD in 2009. The treatment begins with MRI and CT scans of the brain, which doctors use to identify the particular parts of the brain to be targeted for the procedure. Electrodes are then placed at those locations in the brain, and wires are run under the skin to a battery-powered electronic box implanted below the patient's collarbone. This box, known as a pulse generator, sends electrical signals to the electrodes in the brain, similar to the way a pacemaker sends electrical pulses to the heart. Using a wireless controller, a doctor programs the pulse generator to fine-tune the signals. "During the

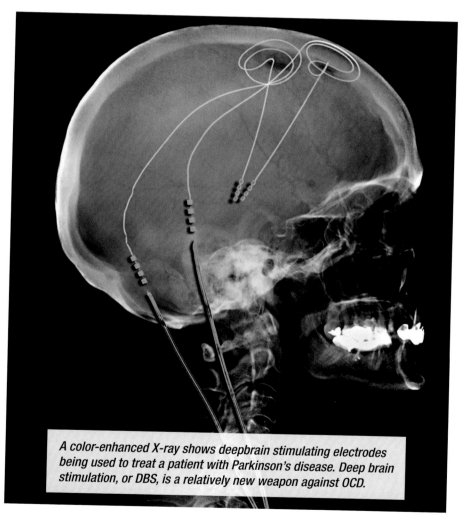

A color-enhanced X-ray shows deepbrain stimulating electrodes being used to treat a patient with Parkinson's disease. Deep brain stimulation, or DBS, is a relatively new weapon against OCD.

programming," explains Rachel A. Davis, a professor at the University of Colorado hospital where Blank had his operation, "we walk through many, many combinations of different settings to try to find where the person has the best response."[23]

Blank actually had three surgeries to place electrodes in his brain, insert two pulse generators, and then connect the components via wires under his skin. After his operations, Blank's OCD began to improve. "That feels good. I love it!"[24] he exclaimed as Davis adjusted the pulse generator shortly after the surgeries. Some two years after his operations, Blank's OCD has greatly improved; he has his own wireless DBS controller so that he can adjust the implants himself. And he is back enjoying great Colorado snowboarding. "I guess, in the end," Blank says, "I kind of feel like I just realized this is probably what happiness feels some-

OCD Case Study: Beth

Beth's OCD began in childhood, but years later her symptoms were brought under control by therapy and medication. At age seventeen she tells her story on the Bay Area OCD and Anxiety Center blog.

Once I was officially diagnosed with OCD, the real work began. My therapist and I created fear hierarchies for my obsessions, as well as one for my phobia. We began to complete the least anxiety-provoking items on the list and gradually worked our way up. Unfortunately, my anxiety was just too high and resilient for CBT to work on its own. I had to look for additional support to really be able to tackle this.

I had been extremely reluctant to take any medication, but eventually I decided to try an SSRI. I was scared that it would change who I was as a person, or that I would have bad side effects, or that I would be dependent on it for life. Today, my only regret is that I didn't try it sooner. My quality of life is so drastically improved that it sometimes feels like a miracle. I no longer have intrusive thoughts, and I don't constantly worry about feeling sick. I went from extreme depression to the happy, stable, motivated person that OCD was holding me back from becoming.

Quoted in DrJenks, "'Beth's' OCD Story: Age 17, POCD, Emetophobia, HOCD, ERP, Medication," Bay Area OCD and Anxiety Center, March 19, 2014. https://bayareaocd.com.

what pretty close to. I haven't been happy in such a long time, and to feel that is a real joy."[25]

Advanced Intervention

According to the *Indian Journal of Psychiatry*, up to 40 percent of OCD patients who undergo psychotherapy, medication, or DBS find that these methods are not effective in relieving their symptoms. There can be many reasons for this, from a patient having a poor relationship with his or her therapist, to drugs that may interfere with a patient's current medications, or even a genetic irregularity that prevents effective treatment. An OCD sufferer who has not responded to the standard therapies is said to have treatment-resistant or refractory OCD. "There are really severe cases of OCD," notes University of Arizona psychiatrist James Wilcox, "where people are incapacitated by their intrusive thoughts and rituals. It's one of the few areas where psychosurgery is still done."[26]

For these individuals, several types of psychosurgical treatments have been shown to be effective for OCD. Anterior capsulotomy and anterior cingulotomy are brain surgeries that are used when all other methods have failed to achieve results. Unlike DBS, in which electrodes are placed in the brain, these surgeries actually alter the structure of the brain at predetermined points to alleviate OCD symptoms. In both procedures, small holes are drilled in the skull and a probe inserted through them into the brain, guided by MRI scans. Surgeons create lesions, or damaged areas, in the brain using heat from an electrode or laser (a process called ablation) or by freezing or cutting. These lesions destroy a specific part of the brain that is connected with OCD, resulting in an improvement of severe OCD symptoms.

"There are really severe cases of OCD where people are incapacitated by their intrusive thoughts and rituals. It's one of the few areas where psychosurgery is still done."[26]

—James Wilcox, psychiatrist

A newer method for treating OCD is the use of a device called a Gamma Knife to create lesions in the brain. The Gamma Knife was invented in Stockholm, Sweden, in 1967. It is not really a knife but a device that uses radiation called gamma rays to treat tumors and other abnormalities in the brain. The use of radioactive cobalt to generate the gamma rays led to this type of therapy being called radiosurgery. The Gamma Knife was first used to treat patients with refractory OCD and other anxiety disorders in 1976. Unlike anterior capsulotomies and cingulotomies, the Gamma Knife is a noninvasive procedure: no holes need to be drilled in the skull. Nearly two hundred beams of gamma radiation penetrate the skull and are focused on a spot in the brain, guided by MRI images. Individually, each beam is too weak to harm the brain, but at the point where they are concentrated, they are col-

Hospitalization may be necessary when individuals are at risk of harming themselves or others. Hospitals have therapists, physicians, and nurses available around the clock to provide support for those severely impaired by OCD.

lectively strong enough to create a lesion. The procedure is painless and completed in one day, with only minor side effects such as headaches and dizziness reported by some patients.

Transcranial Magnetic Stimulation

Another noninvasive treatment for OCD involves the use of magnetic fields to alter brain functions. Transcranial magnetic stimulation (TMS) was developed in the mid-1980s for diagnostic use. It received approval from the FDA in 2008 for treatment of brain disorders such as depression. The FDA approved the use of TMS for OCD treatment in 2018.

TMS is based on a process called magnetic induction: when a rapidly changing electrical current is applied to a coil of wire, it produces a magnetic field. In TMS therapy for OCD, an electromagnetic coil is placed on the patient's head. When activated, the coil generates a magnetic field that passes through the skull and into the brain to a depth of up to 2 inches (5.08 cm). The field produces small electrical currents in the brain, similar to those generated by the probes used in DBS therapy (but without opening the skull). The currents are sent in pulses rather than in a continuous stream, giving the procedure its technical name: repetitive transcranial magnetic stimulation (rTMS).

The currents stimulate the activity of the brain's neural connections, helping alleviate the symptoms of OCD. A session of rTMS can last thirty to sixty minutes, after which the individual can go about normal daily activities. Side effects are mild; they can include headaches and scalp irritation.

While DBS, Gamma Knife, and rTMS procedures are generally outpatient treatments, in the most severe cases of OCD, hospitalization may be necessary. OCD sufferers who may pose a threat to themselves or others, are incapable of caring for their own basic needs, or have suicidal thoughts may be candidates for inpatient programs. In the hospital, there are therapists, physicians, and nurses available around the clock to provide support for those severely impaired by OCD. Treatment may last from several weeks to several months, and cost becomes a major consideration as to whether this type of treatment is feasible.

The many available psychological, medical, and surgical options for treating OCD bring new hope for those who may have previously suffered in silence. But as effective as these treatments are, people with OCD understand that their condition presents a lifelong struggle and that they must create ways to live with and manage their disorder.

Chapter Four

Living with OCD

Amanda Seyfried is an actress who has enjoyed a successful career in film and television since age fourteen. She began her public life early as an eleven-year-old model. Seyfried then found acting work in television soap operas and eventually starred in films such as *Mean Girls*, *Mamma Mia!*, and *Les Misérables*. She was nominated for an Academy Award for Best Supporting Actress in 2021 for the film *Mank*. Seyfried may seem to have it all, but she also has something else: OCD. "I was obsessive as a little girl," she says. "I would have to be really organized—too organized. Things like straightening my room didn't feel right to me; I'd have to redo it and redo it."[27]

Seyfried has been taking antianxiety medication since age nineteen to keep her OCD under control. But she also admits that her OCD gives her a bit of an edge that she uses in her acting. Seyfried has developed a healthy outlook about her disorder. She says:

> A mental illness is a thing that people cast in a different category [from other illnesses], but I don't think it is. It should be taken as seriously as anything else. You don't see the mental illness: It's not a mass; it's not a cyst. But it's there. Why do you need to prove it? If you can treat it, you treat it.

. . . As I get older, the compulsive thoughts and fears have diminished a lot. Knowing that a lot of my fears are not reality-based really helps.[28]

Seyfried is coping honestly with her OCD, acknowledging the reality of the disorder and her need to continue her medication. But arriving at that point in an OCD sufferer's life can be a difficult hurdle to conquer.

Insight into OCD

When people fall ill due to an illness caused by a viral or bacterial infection, they usually know that they are sick. Fever, pain, upset stomach, and other symptoms make it abundantly clear that something is wrong, and if they are serious enough, medical attention may be required. People with OCD, however, may not recognize that their symptoms indicate an illness. The process that enables people to reach the conclusion that they have a mental illness is known as insight. This is the ability to evaluate external reality and to assess one's own problems or personality traits.

Determining whether an individual has insight is an essential part of diagnosing and treating OCD. There are three levels of insight that therapists use during an evaluation for OCD: fair to good insight into the disorder, poor insight, or absent/delusional insight. OCD sufferers who understand that the thoughts that cause their obsessions are likely or definitely not true and that their compulsions have no effect in combating these intrusive thoughts are said to have fair to good insight into their disorder. Individuals with poor insight believe that their thoughts are probably true, and those with absent or delusional insight are convinced that the thoughts they experience are absolutely true. These categories of insight

"As I get older, the compulsive thoughts and fears have diminished a lot. Knowing that a lot of my fears are not reality-based really helps."[28]

—Amanda Seyfried, actress

can occur in any type of OCD, whether mild or severe. In addition, individuals with poor or absent insight may not grasp the extent to which OCD affects their daily lives.

Janet Singer's son Dan suffered from such profound OCD that he could barely eat. Although his mother was at first baffled by his behavior, Dan was able to gain good insight into his disorder by searching the internet. The information he found online was confirmed by his doctor. This knowledge helped Dan through rigorous therapy and learning to cope with his OCD, as Janet, an author of books on the disorder, explains. "Having insight can be invaluable when in treatment for OCD," she says. "I've previously written about Dan's journey where I've noted that just being made aware of

Actress Amanda Seyfried has enjoyed a successful career in film and television. She has spoken publicly about her OCD and how hard she has worked, through treatment, to lead a normal life.

his cognitive distortions, or the tricks OCD can play, was extremely helpful in his fight against OCD. And insight doesn't always have to come naturally. It can be helped along by a good therapist."[29]

OCD sufferers with poor insight often delay treatment for their disorder. They may not be motivated enough to seek out a therapist, and if they do, they may not attend therapy sessions as required or take prescribed medication. While therapy can help increase an individual's insight into his or her OCD, it takes time to see results.

Fighting the Stigma of OCD

One of the biggest obstacles to living a normal life with OCD is the stigma often attached to OCD and mental illness in general. This stigma results from the attitudes of people who do not understand the seriousness of OCD and who stereotype its sufferers as different, bad, or somehow responsible for their own illness. This disparaging of OCD sufferers can lead them to internalize (or self-stigmatize) their shame and embarrassment, to the point that they begin to believe that they really are bad people and have

Offhand Comments

It is a seemingly harmless offhand phrase that many people toss off when they are having a bad day or difficulty keeping their priorities straight. "I'm so OCD about keeping my stuff organized," someone may say. Or, "I get OCD about studying when I have a test the next day." It is even used as a joke when, for example, the phrase "OCD: Obsessive Christmas Disorder" is printed on a holiday sweatshirt. The problem is that when such a phrase is casually used, it displays an ignorance of the serious challenges that OCD creates in sufferers' lives.

OCD is, in fact, a mental illness, and those who have it struggle daily with its hold on their mind and life. As one student with OCD notes, "When people who are not diagnosed with this condition say things like 'OMG, I'm so OCD,' in addition to being grammatically incorrect (you can't be a disorder, you have one), you are belittling and undermining a very serious mental condition that plagues many. To say you suffer from it when you don't is to invalidate those who actually battle it every day."

Theupdateecolint, "OMG, I'm So OCD!," The Update, June 4, 2017. https://thelachatupdate.com.

brought their disorder on themselves. Even families of OCD sufferers can experience the stigma associated with the disorder.

Stigmatization of OCD can cause increased anxiety in people with the disorder. They may fear that they could lose their job or have trouble with personal relationships if their condition was made known. To cope with this fear, OCD sufferers may spend time and energy attempting to hide the fact that they suffer from a mental illness. Coulter has experience in concealing OCD symptoms. She says:

> "Take the anxiety that's at the heart of OCD and add the stress of trying to keep your symptoms a secret—it's draining beyond belief."[30]
>
> —Anne Coulter, OCD sufferer

Hiding OCD symptoms . . . requires an incredible amount of energy. Those of us who have it often become terrific actors. We're so busy trying to make sure other people don't notice the odd things we're doing that we actually come up with rituals to hide the rituals! I never wanted anyone to realize that I was checking something to the point of obsession. Take the anxiety that's at the heart of OCD and add the stress of trying to keep your symptoms a secret—it's draining beyond belief.[30]

There are several ways to combat the stigma of OCD. Seeking professional help is probably the single most important aspect of keeping OCD under control. Involving family and friends in the process will provide a support group to turn to when self-stigma begins to take over. OCD sufferers who educate themselves about the disorder not only help themselves but can spread accurate information to others in an effort to reduce the misconceptions about OCD that lead to stigmatizing behavior.

OCD in School

Elementary-school-age children who have OCD have an especially difficult time understanding the nature of their disorder. They may be ashamed of the rituals they perform in order to relieve the stress of their obsessions and embarrassed when they do these rituals in class. The stress of having OCD can have a devastating effect on a student's performance in school.

In their book *Obsessive-Compulsive Disorder*, counselor Bruce M. Hyman and registered nurse Cherry Pedrick relate the story of Alex, a straight-A elementary school student. Alex was always meticulous in his schoolwork, and his assignments showed his careful attention to detail. By the time he was in junior high, however, Alex began struggling. According to Hyman and Pedrick, Alex "fell behind on his homework and his grades went from As to Bs and Cs. It wasn't that he couldn't do the work; he just didn't have time to complete it."[31] Alex was obsessed with checking his work again and again to make sure there were no errors. He rarely finished tests, and he lost sleep staying up late to perfect his homework. The more his grades fell, the more Alex felt anxious and stressed. Eventually, Alex was diagnosed with OCD.

There are thousands of kids like Alex whose schoolwork is

Although getting professional help is key to managing OCD, talking openly with family and friends can provide needed support for those moments when anxiety and shame resurface.

negatively affected by OCD. Smart and competent students may lose the ability to concentrate on their studies because of anxiety caused by their obsessions and compulsions. Tardiness, the inability to complete assignments, a constant need for reassurance, and obsessively arranging and rearranging paper, pens and pencils, and other desk items are all indications of OCD in the classroom.

Psychologists have found that it is helpful to have a child externalize his or her obsessions. Giving obsessions an identity, such as thinking of them as being caused by a wicked gremlin or endowing them with a ridiculous name, can help children gain a sense of power over their disorder. By separating themselves from their obsessions, children come to realize that what is causing their anxiety is not their fault but something that has "invaded" their consciousness. As with adults who have OCD, children can learn to keep their OCD under control with professional counseling and possibly medication.

Living with Uncertainty

An old adage says that there is nothing certain in life but death and taxes. As simplistic as that may be, the truth is that we live in a world filled with uncertainty. Most people are able to handle this uncertainty and still function in everyday life. But for individuals with OCD, uncertainty can be a daunting roadblock to a normal life. "OCD is known as the 'doubting disease,'" says OCD sufferer Cara Rothenberg. "It makes you doubt everything you know, everyone you love, and everything you are."[32]

With OCD, nagging uncertainty affects every aspect of daily life. Is the front door really locked? OCD says: maybe not, better check it again. Did you wash your hands thoroughly enough? OCD: No harm in doing it again—and again and again. If the compulsions are performed enough times and in the right way, eventually the anxiety caused by the obsessions will lessen and daily activities can resume—until the next obsession takes hold. At least that is what OCD demands. The problem is that uncertainty

There's an App for OCD

Stephen Smith was a quarterback for his college football team and a good student with a bright future until OCD sidelined him and left his life in turmoil. He eventually got better through therapy but wondered why it was so difficult and time-consuming to find help. That is when he and several colleagues created NOCD. The NOCD app gives OCD sufferers easy access to life-changing therapy.

NOCD works by matching people with OCD to professionals who guide them through personalized live video therapy sessions. The therapists specialize in exposure and response prevention techniques that have proved most effective in treating OCD. The app has self-help tools for support between online sessions. "We know from clinical research," says Smith, "that there are clear, easy-to-follow protocols that work for people with OCD. NOCD puts this science into action with a consumer-friendly interface that brings these tools from a doctor's office to your phone." NOCD is available for both iOS and Android devices.

There are many other resources that provide help for individuals with OCD, including apps for evaluating possible OCD symptoms, encouraging positive thoughts, tracking goals and therapy progress, and connecting with peers and other support groups.

Quoted in Jackie Pilossoph, "Northbrook Native Launches App to Help OCD Patients," *Chicago Tribune*, March 23, 2016. www.chicagotribune.com.

can never be completely eliminated from life. Most people without OCD realize that nothing is perfect, and people can never know everything that can or may happen in their lives. But for those with OCD, uncertainty can be debilitating.

"Certainty is a myth," says Michael Tompkins, codirector of the San Francisco Bay Area Center for Cognitive Therapy, "a comforting myth but a myth nonetheless. . . . Acceptance or tolerance of uncertainty is the heart of any plan to recover from OCD."[33] One way to accept uncertainty is through a process called habituation, which means that an individual's response to a stimulus begins to decrease the more he or she encounters it. For example, the ticking of a newly purchased clock can be annoying at first, but in a few days or weeks the ticks are hardly noticeable. In the same way, the more an OCD sufferer learns to endure intrusive thoughts without responding, the less anxiety those thoughts will produce. Habituation is the basis of ERP therapy. "Once you've gone through ERP therapy," says Shala Nicely, "you have a black belt in managing uncertainty. With that black belt, you can manage the everyday uncertainties of life even better than people who don't have OCD and who haven't been through exposure therapy."[34]

Learning to accept uncertainty is hard, even for those who learn ways through therapy to confront and accept obsessions and not give in to compulsions. In their efforts to spend less energy worrying about things to come, many people with OCD have found additional help through the practice of mindfulness.

Mindfulness and OCD

Mindfulness is the concept of being aware of living for the present, a way of appreciating life as it happens in the moment, in a nonjudgmental way. Eating in a mindful way, for instance, means noticing the tastes, textures, temperatures, and flavors of the food being consumed, rather than letting the mind wander to other concerns. As another example, while driving, a mindful person will notice the scenery, the music playing on the radio, and the comfort of the car's air-conditioning rather than worrying about possibly being late for an appointment.

An attitude of mindfulness allows OCD sufferers to coexist with an intrusive thought without letting it take over. They can accept the thought while not judging it or trying to defeat it through compulsions. To learn how to use mindfulness, OCD sufferers are encouraged to practice observing life around them. It is also helpful to cultivate a healthy lifestyle that includes exercise, eating right, and fostering an attitude of not judging everything and everyone. Mindfulness techniques can include deep breathing exercises, muscle relaxation, meditation, and focusing on self-esteem. Jon Kabat-Zinn, the founder of a program known as mindfulness-based stress reduction, concisely sums up mindfulness in a way that can be especially meaningful for OCD sufferers: "You can't stop the waves, but you can learn to surf."[35]

Life with OCD

There are probably as many stories of how to live with OCD as there are people with the disorder. College student Haley Hutchinson tells about her life with OCD after undergoing therapy:

> I have come to accept that I will never completely overcome the obsessive-compulsive disorder, but I have learned what it means to be a fighter and overcome fear. . . . I used to feel ashamed of my OCD, like it was some tremendous secret I needed to protect. I have come to realize that I am not defined by a diagnosis, nor am I guilty about who I am. My struggles have made me into the woman I am today.[36]

The struggles of OCD sufferers can be extremely frustrating. Mark Highet lives in Queensland, Australia, and has OCD. He says:

> The three things that are the hardest for me are the guilt of having it, the shame of trying to hide it and the humiliation when someone sees you. I had to pull all my workmates aside and say, this is hard for me and I'm sorry you have to see me repeating things. . . . It's not rational, it's not reasonable. It's against my will and I don't want to do it. It feels like I'm so busy trying to live, that I'm forgetting to live.[37]

"I used to feel ashamed of my OCD, like it was some tremendous secret I needed to protect. I have come to realize that I am not defined by a diagnosis, nor am I guilty about who I am."[36]

—Haley Hutchinson, OCD sufferer

As difficult as it is to live with a disorder that has no cure, there is hope for individuals with OCD. Grammy Award–nominated singer Camila Cabello worked hard at CBT, breathing exercises, and overall care for her health and self-esteem to combat her OCD. "I feel the healthi-

Grammy Award–nominated singer Camila Cabello has been able to manage her OCD with CBT, breathing exercises, and overall care for her health and self-esteem. Although she sometimes still has anxiety, she rarely experiences the symptoms of OCD.

est and most connected to myself I've ever been," she says, "and nowadays I seldom suffer from OCD symptoms. Anxiety comes and goes, but now it feels like just another difficult emotion, as opposed to something that's consuming my life. By doing the work and showing up for myself every day, I feel like I have more trust in myself than ever before."[38]

Having a chronic disorder means constant vigilance and a lifetime of dedication to do whatever is necessary to control that disease. Most people understand that chronic physical illnesses need constant maintenance. Individuals with diabetes, for example, must frequently monitor their blood sugar levels and self-administer insulin to keep the glucose in their bodies at the proper levels. Coping with heart disease in its many forms usually requires lifestyle changes such as getting proper exercise, eating right, and having regular checkups. OCD falls into the category of chronic disorders that need continual maintenance. Drugs prescribed for OCD may have to be taken for the rest of a sufferer's life, and cognitive therapy exercises must continue even after professional sessions end. Confronting obsessions without resorting to temporary relief through compulsions is a difficult but necessary skill to master.

As with any chronic illness, living with OCD can be challenging. But the goal of having a nearly normal life in the face of the uncertainty, guilt, and stigma associated with OCD is worth pursuing.

Introduction: Ben's Story

1. Quoted in Child Mind Institute, "A 13-Year-Old Learns to Fight OCD," 2021. www.childmind.org.
2. Quoted in Child Mind Institute, "A 13-Year-Old Learns to Fight OCD."
3. Quoted in Child Mind Institute, "A 13-Year-Old Learns to Fight OCD."
4. Shala Nicely, "Why There's No Cure for OCD," *Beyond the Doubt* (blog), *Psychology Today*, April 13, 2018. www.psychologytoday.com.

Chapter One: What Is OCD?

5. Emma, "My OCD Story," Mind, January 16, 2019. www.mind.org.uk.
6. Nicely, "Why There's No Cure for OCD."
7. Maya, "OCD: A Patient's Journey Forward," Biohaven Pharmaceuticals, December 8, 2020. www.ocdtrial.org.
8. American Psychiatric Association, *Diagnostic and Statistical Manual of Mental Disorders*, 5th ed. Washington, DC: American Psychiatric Association, 2013, p. 237.
9. Modern Therapy, "Differences in OCD and Perfectionism," July 18, 2018. https://moderntherapy.online.

Chapter Two: The Causes of OCD

10. Quoted in Kara Gavin, "Stuck in a Loop of 'Wrongness': Brain Study Shows Roots of OCD," Michigan Medicine, November 29, 2018. https://labblog.uofmhealth.org.
11. Quoted in Peter Dockrill, "Researchers Have Finally Discovered Genes That Are Linked to OCD," ScienceAlert, October 21, 2017. www.sciencealert.com.
12. Quoted in Alice Klein, "Four Brain Genes Help Explain Obsessive Compulsive Disorder," *New Scientist*, October 17, 2017. www.newscientist.com.

13. Quoted in Ashley Laderer, "Yes, OCD Is Genetic but Having a Parent or Sibling with OCD Doesn't Guarantee You'll Have It," Insider, September 18, 2020. www.insider.com.
14. Cheryl Carmin, *Obsessive-Compulsive Disorder Demystified: An Essential Guide for Understanding and Living with OCD*. Cambridge, MA: Da Capo, 2009, p. 57.
15. Quoted in John S. March and Christine M. Benton, *Talking Back to OCD*. New York: Guilford, 2007, p. 16.
16. Quoted in Michael A. Tompkins, *OCD: A Guide for the Newly Diagnosed*. Oakland, CA: New Harbinger, 2012, p. 31.

Chapter Three: Treating OCD
17. Nicely, "Why There's No Cure for OCD."
18. Quoted in Carmin, *Obsessive-Compulsive Disorder Demystified*, p. 77.
19. Quoted in Carmin, *Obsessive-Compulsive Disorder Demystified*, p. 110.
20. Quoted in Carmin, *Obsessive-Compulsive Disorder Demystified*, pp. 111, 157.
21. Quoted in Anna Bella Zawahir, "Combined CBT, SSRI Treatment May Be More Effective for OCD," Psychiatry Advisor, May 17, 2019. www.psychiatyradvisor.com.
22. Quoted in Best of Us, *Jon Blank: From Brain Surgery to the Back-Country—Obsessive-Compulsive Disorder*, YouTube, August 7, 2019. www.youtube.com/watch?v=wYLJGuUt4iI.
23. Quoted in Best of Us, *Jon Blank*.
24. Quoted in Todd Neff, "Deep Brain Stimulation Zaps OCD, Opens New Path for Young Patient," UC Health, December 19, 2019. www.uchealth.org.
25. Quoted in Best of Us, *Jon Blank*.
26. Quoted in Nick Stockton, "Psychosurgeons Use Lasers to Burn Away Mental Illness," *Wired*, June 25, 2015. www.wired.com.

Chapter Four: Living with OCD
27. Quoted in Paul Cavaco, "Amanda Seyfried: Her *Allure* Photo Shoot," *Allure*, August 16, 2009. www.allure.com.
28. Quoted in David Denicolo, "Amanda Seyfried on Her Mental Health, Her Dog, and Those Eyes," *Allure*, October 18, 2016. www.allure.com.
29. Janet Singer, "OCD and Insight," Psych Central, May 17, 2016. www.psychcentral.com.

30. Quoted in Carmin, *Obsessive-Compulsive Disorder Demystified*, p. xii.
31. Bruce M. Hyman and Cherry Pedrick, *Obsessive-Compulsive Disorder*. Brookfield, CT: Twenty-First Century, 2003, p. 17.
32. Quoted in Patrick Carey, "A Pretty Spectacular View: Keeping OCD in Perspective," NOCD, February 21, 2018. www.treatmyocd.com.
33. Tompkins, *OCD*, p. 94.
34. Nicely, "Why There's No Cure for OCD."
35. Quoted in Calvin Holbrook, "Mindfulness Quotes: 10 Sayings to Inspire and Ground You," Happiness. www.happiness.com.
36. Haley Hutchinson, "Living with Severe Obsessive-Compulsive Disorder," *Middlebury Campus*, October 8, 2020. www.middlebury campus.com.
37. Quoted in Queensland Health, "What Is It Like to Live with Obsessive Compulsive Disorder?," October 10, 2018. www.health.qld .gov.au.
38. Camila Cabello, "How Camila Cabello Became Friends with Her Anxiety," *WSJ Magazine*, May 28, 2020. www.wsj.com.

Getting Help and Information

Anxiety and Depression Association of America (ADAA)

www.adaa.org

The ADAA's mission is to help provide a better quality of life for those suffering from anxiety disorders, which include OCD, post-traumatic stress disorder, and other co-occurring disorders. The organization's website includes help in finding a therapist, articles on coping with adolescent anxiety, and a webinar to help kids and teens understand their OCD.

International OCD Foundation (IOCDF)

www.iocdf.org

The mission of the IOCDF is to raise awareness of OCD and provide resources for those who suffer from the disorder. The IOCDF organizes local events, many of which are aimed at teen OCD sufferers. Its website includes a link to an interactive comic about OCD.

National Alliance on Mental Illness (NAMI)

www.nami.org

The NAMI is a grassroots mental health organization with over six hundred local affiliates that provide support, education, and resources at the local level. It provides a free helpline for people with OCD and other mental disorders, as well as a web page specifically for teens and young adults.

National Institute of Mental Health (NIMH)

www.nimh.nih.gov

The NIMH is a federal agency that conducts research on mental disorders under the guidance of the National Institutes of Health. Its website offers brochures and fact sheets on all types of mental illnesses and has links to articles of special interest to teens.

For Further Research

Books

Jonathan S. Abramowitz, *Getting Over OCD: A 10-Step Workbook for Taking Back Your Life*. New York: Guilford, 2018.

Michelle Garcia Andersen, *Living with OCD*. San Diego, CA: ReferencePoint, 2019.

Jon Hershfield and Shala Nicely, *Everyday Mindfulness for OCD: Tricks & Skills for Living Joyfully*. Oakland, CA: New Harbinger, 2017.

Christine Honders, *OCD: The Struggle with Obsessions and Compulsions*. New York: Lucent, 2018.

Shala Nicely, *Is Fred in the Refrigerator?* Marietta, GA: Nicely Done, 2018.

Ben Sedley and Lisa Coyne, *Stuff That's Loud: A Teen's Guide to Unspiraling When OCD Gets Noisy*. Oakland, CA: Instant Help, 2020.

Barbara Sheen, *Teens and OCD*. San Diego, CA: ReferencePoint, 2017.

Internet Sources

Beyond OCD, "Just for Teens," 2019. https://beyondocd.org.

Bethany Bray, "Living with—and Beyond—OCD," *Counseling Today*, January 24, 2020. https://ct.counseling.org.

Benjamin Cohen, "Living with OCD: One Student's Story," Buzz Magazines, May 31, 2018. https://thebuzzmagazines.com.

Shayla Love, "19 Everyday Things That Trigger My OCD," *Vice*, May 30, 2018. www.vice.com.

Teen OCD Podcast, "My OCD Story." https://open.spotify.com.

Index

Picture Credits

Cover: Athanasia Nomikou/Shutterstock

Craig E. Blohm has written numerous books and maga-zine articles for young readers. He and his wife, Desiree, reside in Tinley Park, Illinois.